HAPPY "5th" BIRTHDAY
BLAKE.

AMIGO

LOVE GIGI + G-PA
LIGHTLE.

For my grandchildren.

Acknowledgements

Jeska, my illustrator, who made it possible for my book to be published.

My husband, for his love and support.

Gladys, for her help and support along the way.

Written by: Charlene Owens
Illustrated by: Jeska R

Published in Canada by Charlene Owens, 2024

ISBN: 978-1-0690631-0-6xt S

Amigo loved to prance and dance in the field.

He liked to run across the field jumping over branches and streams.

One day, Amigo approached a log that had fallen across the path.

He peered at it, then backed up,

took a deep breath, and ran as fast as he could to jump and soar through the air, just like the horses.

But Amigo didn't jump high enough. His legs were too short.

His hooves hit the log and he fell to the ground.

He scrambled to his feet hoping no one had seen him.

He watched the horses prancing and dancing. Their smooth, shiny coats glistened in the sun.

He watched as they flew easily over the same log that he had tripped over.

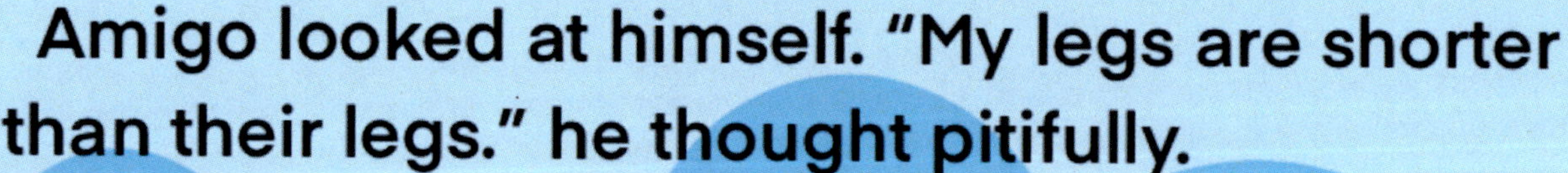

Amigo looked at himself. "My legs are shorter than their legs." he thought pitifully.

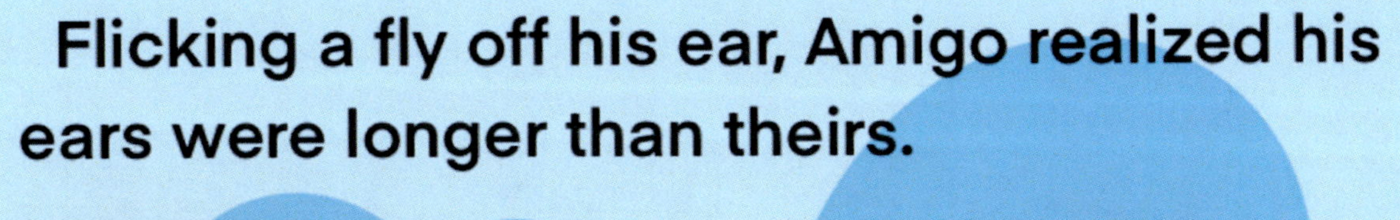

Flicking a fly off his ear, Amigo realized his ears were longer than theirs.

He noticed his coat was rough and shaggy. Not smooth and shiny.

A terrible thought came to him. Perhaps I am not a horse at all!

He opened his mouth to neigh in despair. But instead of a neigh, out came a loud HEE HAAW!

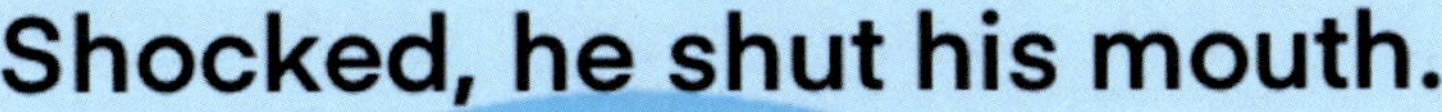

Shocked, he shut his mouth.

Amigo spent the night feeling sad.

He couldn't jump like a horse because his legs were too short. His ears were too long, his coat was too shaggy, and he made a dreadful sound when he opened his mouth. "If I am not a horse, I am not good enough," he decided.

The next day the sky grew dark and a huge storm blew in. Amigo's ears twitched with the rumble of thunder.

The sky lit up and the rain crashed down as if it were beating on a drum.

The sides of the old barn shook as the wind roared, causing the barn to creak and groan.

The storm didn't bother Amigo. He stood outside, savoring the smell of rain.

He could hear the horses inside the barn, stomping and clomping in their stalls. He heard their frightened cries as they tried to break free.

A boy stood at the door of the barn. "Come on Amigo, it's time for you to come inside. The horses need you!"

Sighing, Amigo trotted toward the barn, where the horses neighed, reared and stomped in their stalls.

As soon as Amigo entered the barn, the horses' heads turned toward him. Slowly, they calmed down. The boy was right. They no longer neighed and reared. Their hooves no longer stomped in the stalls.

Amigo's ears perked up. "The horses need me!" he thought. "My presence helps them when they're afraid!"

"You are the best donkey in the world," the boy exclaimed as he flung his arms around Amigo.

"I may not have long legs, or small ears, or a soft shiny coat like a horse," reasoned Amigo. "I may bray instead of neigh, but that's alright, because I am not a horse." And then Amigo knew.

"I am a donkey and donkeys are good enough!"

Facts About Donkeys

1. Other names for donkeys are burro, jackass, and ass.
2. A male donkey is referred to as Jack and the female as Jenny.
3. Donkeys do not like to live alone because they get lonely. They live with herds of sheep or goats. When the donkey has bonded with the herd, the donkey will protect the herd against predators.
4. Donkeys have large ears and can hear another donkey from sixty miles away.
5. Their ears help them keep cool when the weather is hot.
6. Donkeys hate the rain. Their coat is not waterproof.
7. Humans need to earn a donkey's trust before training it.
8. Donkeys do not like to run.
9. Donkeys are known to have a calming effect on horses. They have a patient and kind nature.
10. Donkeys live for around twenty-five to thirty years in the wild, and up to forty if they have been looked after.

Did you see me walk through every page of Amigo's *journey?*

Works Cited

Baidy, Sankalan. "30 interesting Donkey facts." Facts Legend. May 22, 2015. factslegend.org/30-interesting-donkey-facts/#.Jan30, 2019.

Bradford, Alina. "Facts About Donkeys." Live Science Contributor. March 31, 2016. livescience.com/54258-donkeys.html

"Why Do People Keep Donkeys?" Donkeys. ypte Young People's Trust For The Environment. 2019. ypte.org.uk/factsheets/donkey/why-do-people-keep-donkeys. Jan 30, 2019

Manufactured by Amazon.ca
Bolton, ON